God Belongs In My City™

Jack Redmond and Daniel Sanabria

God Belongs In My City™

ISBN: 978-1-937514-02-0

Printed in the United States of America
God Belongs In My City™

About the Authors

Daniel Sanabria is the Youth Pastor at Park Slope Christian Tabernacle in Brooklyn, NY. He is the cofounder of God Belongs In My City™ – www.Godbelongsinmycity.com. He has also served the youth of New York City as a cofounder of Urban Kingdom Youth Ministries – www.urbankingdomym.com.

Jack Redmond is the founder of Fourth Generation Ministries – www.4thgen.org. He has also served for over ten years as the Youth Pastor of Christ Church in Montclair and Rockaway, New Jersey. Jack also has a weekly radio program entitled: *INFUSION*.

Also Written by Jack Redmond

INFUSION: Receive. Grow. Give it Away…

Wounded Heart: Keys to Overcoming Life's Pain and Disappointments

People Matter to God: Experiencing Personal Transformation and Sharing It with Others

Endorsements

Daniel Sanabria truly heard God's heart cry for New York City and the cities of our country and the world when he wrote down the words: ***"God Belongs In My City"***. What started as a one-day prayer march has already gone throughout many cities in the United States. God belongs in our cities, and I believe that this movement will touch countless lives and impact many cities in the days to come!

Ron Luce
President and Founder of Teen Mania Ministries
Author of ***Friends Without Benefits*** and
BATTLE CRY for a Generation

Right now, over half the world's population lives in cities and over 60 percent of those are eighteen years old or younger. Wouldn't if be great if God poured out His Spirit in these last days and we were able to see REVIVAL come to our cities? Youth, prayer, and unity have always been at the core of spiritual awakenings! I believe that God is once again using youth and prayer through the ***God Belongs In My City*** movement to unite Christ followers and to prepare the way for His merciful outpouring..."for such a time as this!"

TRAINING LEADERS,
WHO TRAIN LEADERS,
WHO TRANSFORM YOUTH

URBAN YOUTH WORKERS INSTITUTE
Larry Acosta, President & Founder

I believe that ***God Belongs In My City*** is what true ministry is about. Danny had the courage to do what many youth leaders have trouble doing. He allowed his youth to come up with an idea based on their righteous anger over an atheist movement and gave them the room to do something about it. He empowered them to act on their convictions and create a movement never seen in New York City before. Danny Sanabria is a great example of a youth leader getting out of the way, having confidence in his youth, and even if they failed, being courageous enough to give them the liberty to learn from the failure.

Thank God ***GBIMC*** was a huge success for Danny and his youth.

David Serrano
Youth Development Specialist | U.S. Programs |
World Vision New York

Dedication Page

In 2009, I never expected God to do such a grand thing as birth a vision like ***God Belongs In My City*** in the hearts of my leaders and myself. All praise and glory be unto HIS name because He is truly the only one deserving of it.

I'd like to dedicate this book to my wife, Diane, who is my partner, my love, and my lifelong best friend. It's so nice to know that I don't have to look behind me to know you're there. All I need to do is look beside me because that's where you are. Having you by my side is the greatest blessing God could have ever given me. I love you!

I'd also like to dedicate this book to my loving family and friends. Thank you Dad, Mom, Jon, Lilly, Steven, Dorothy, Timothy, Maria, Herbert, Phillip, Jeremy, and my awesome niece and nephews Isabella, Caleb, Nathan, and David, for being my constant support and for always giving me your wisdom! Thanks for always believing in me.

Thank you Noel, Samantha, and Vanessa for dreaming with me every week as we lead our Crossover Youth Ministry students. Thank you for helping birth and grow ***God Belongs In My City*** to the place it is. Your hard work and dedication does

NOT go unnoticed. You guys are heroes to this generation and I love you dearly.

Thank you to the cities all over the country and the world that have stepped up to be misfits for the cause of Christ! You are changing the atmosphere, changing environments, bringing hope, transforming lives, and brightening the future of generations to come!

Thank you, reader, for allowing us to share one of the most pivotal moments in our lives with you. My prayer is that you are moved to become a world changer and not just talk about change, but actually BE the change that you want to see. God is willing to use you if you are willing to be used.

Last but certainly not least, I want to thank the Urban Kingdom Youth Ministry network partners, youth leaders, and youth of New York City for coming together on November 14, 2009, and October 30, 2010, to proclaim that God belongs in our city. By your actions and dedication, you have set a standard for cities all over the country and the world to take back what the devil has stolen. You all inspire me and give hope that this generation is not a lost cause and that the people of God are about their Father's business. Thank you for grabbing hold of that spirit of unity that is so desperately needed to further God's Kingdom. Press on! Never give up! See you at the next walk!

Pastor Daniel Sanabria

Chapter 1 – The Birth of God Belongs In My City 15
Chapter 2 – You Can Change Your City! 25
Chapter 3 – Prayer, Atheists, and Teens on the Go! 31
Chapter 4 – Healing Our Land Through the Power of Prayer 43
Chapter 5 – Passion, Four Youth Leaders, and a Notebook 51
Chapter 6 – The Body of Christ Rising Up 59
Chapter 7 – Empowering Young People— The Church of Today! 63
Chapter 8 – Encountering New York City 77
Chapter 9 – Aftereffects of GBIMC Prayer Walks 85
Chapter 10 – GBIMC—Spreading to Other Cities 91
Chapter 11 – Pray in Your School; Pray for Your School! 99
Chapter 12 – GBIMC—Adaptable to Any City— Adaptable to YOUR City! 103

Foreword

Goliaths fall when adults like Saul get out of David's way. The biblical figure, David, was an untested teenager, a shepherd boy with no military training. Yet he simultaneously proved to be the only man among soldiers courageous enough to confront the giant, Goliath. For forty days, Goliath's taunts had paralyzed Israel's king and army with fear. Then David overheard the mockery, witnessed the cowardice of the adults around him, and was moved to action. King Saul reluctantly agreed, and the rest, as they say, is history.

I first became gripped by the idea that youth can and must be empowered to lead as a thirteen-year-old on a weekend retreat. My youth pastor challenged one hundred or so teens to find a solitary place for Bible reading and prayer for an hour. Struggling to decide where to start, I remembered hearing that Timothy was a young guy when his mentor, Paul, wrote him a letter. So I read the letter start to finish, and what I found awakened something in me that changed me forever.

> Let no one look down on you because you are young, but set an example to the believers in speech, in conduct, in love, in faith and in purity. (1 Timothy 4:12)

I was blown away. Whitney Houston was still relevant at the time, and her latest, greatest hit said I was the future, not the present! The idea that "youth are the future"—and, therefore, not particularly useful now—was echoed everywhere around me, especially in church. All the important people on Sunday mornings were fully grown. The people my age were segregated to the junior congregation with the junior Holy Spirit, supervised by a couple of adults crazy enough to lead us.

And here the Apostle Paul was challenging me (not just his protégé, Timothy) to let no one look down on me because I was young. To be an example to believers of all ages. To reject adult condescension and actually lead!

Every day since then, in one form or another, I've attempted to empower young people to lead change in their cultures and communities by cultivating their character and competence and then getting out of their way.

Twenty or so years later felt like déjà vu all over again.

Rev. Dr. Raymond Rivera, founder and president of Latino Pastoral Action Center (LPAC) in the Bronx, believes students are essential to efforts to transform communities. In 2009, that conviction motivated LPAC to produce "Kickin' It Old Skool," the first student leadership conference in LPAC's and my collective memory that was actually led by students. Paradoxically, so-called student leadership events typically involve adults teaching students, or adults teaching other adults, how to lead students.

Rarely do adults voluntarily play a supporting role to students leading the event.

Kickin' It stood in stark contrast to this tradition. LPAC empowered twelve student organizers from four New York City boroughs to defy the stereotype and design a leadership event that they and other students would lead, armed with a budget to pull it off. Sixty-eight of their peers gathered for the conference at Washington Irving High School in Manhattan on September 12, 2009, and 175 enjoyed the evening concert as well. Dr. Rivera's message that day: "Share your story. Declare your future. Inspire other students. Remember, tomorrow needs you. Prepare for it today."

Little did he know that two months later, three of the Kickin' It student organizers would rally a dozen or so other students to coordinate **God Belongs In My City *(GBIMC),*** the largest student-led prayer walk in New York City. Fifteen hundred marchers walked a total of eight miles in Manhattan, culminating in a Times Square rally and silent prayer "flash mob" in the main lobby of Grand Central Station.

The catalyst for the day was a dismayed youth pastor who asked some of his student leaders why Christians were publicly silent after atheists launched a citywide ad blitz that October claiming one million New Yorkers reject the existence of God. They responded as only youth can: by launching a movement. Their tools of the trade: Facebook, Twitter, YouTube, and smartphones, social media inventions by their generation for their generation that empowered their efforts.

Less than two weeks later, on November 14, despite a storm bearing down on the Northeast and flash floods forecast throughout the day, fifteen hundred people showed up at the two rally points at 9:00 a.m. God smiled on them. The sun began to shine, and the rains held for four hours, just long enough to complete the walk. They walked with a purpose: to radiate love and affection for God and neighbor, while praying that God would be glorified in our city by lives that love others well.

In the last year and a half, ***God Belongs In My City*** student-led prayer walks have occurred in twenty cities. Over twenty thousand ***GBIMC*** T-shirts have been worn by teens around the country. The ***GBIMC*** story has reverberated at conferences and churches, and catalyzed similar student leadership. And ***GBIMC*** collaborated with 20/20 Vision for Schools to launch a related student-led education reform initiative called ***I Am My School***.

This book tells their story. It's a story of leadership, student leadership, because "God belongs in my city," and God requires students to lead. If you're a young person reading this, be inspired. But don't stay that way. Do something. Pray. Serve. Lead. Catalyze change. If you're an adult reading this, experience the awe and joy that come after we get out of David's way long enough to watch Goliath topple.

Jeremy Del Rio, Esq.
Cofounder and Director of 20/20 Vision for Schools
www.JeremyDelRio.com or www.2020schools.org

Chapter 1

The Birth of God Belongs In My City

We walked from Battery Park to 42nd Street and Times Square, passing through Ground Zero, City Hall, and Union Square, to name just a few major sites in New York City. These were places that as a New Yorker, I had been to at least a thousand times; however, this time I was standing out amongst the crowds of people with a simple statement that did not need to be spoken aloud. There were no tracts, sermons, or altar calls. Our message was quiet and clear. What a rush!

—Rachel-Anne Morales

The events that took place in New York City on November 14, 2009, were not intentional. While the purpose behind the events was thought out, it was never meant to start a movement. Approximately fifteen hundred New York and New Jersey hearts gathered for the cause of Christ. When God belongs in a city, He makes sure that the WHOLE city knows it! This chapter is the story retold in detail by Daniel Sanabria.

In a response to the media posters, signs, and advertisements put up by atheists, three of my young adult leaders gathered with me in my office on November 2, 2009. Together, we decided that something had to change in New York City. These advertisements claimed that people did not need God to be moral or good. They even went as far as to place one sign that stated, "A million New Yorkers are good without God. Are you?" The four of us, being native New Yorkers, felt an immediate "Holy Discontent," as spoken about by Bill Hybels, Senior Pastor at Willow Creek in Illinois. This discontent moved us to brainstorm on how we could combat these ads with the love of Christ.

God Belongs In My City started at a small church with about thirty youth and four youth leaders. Every Monday morning we sit down to discuss the previous week and plan for the week ahead. That morning in the newspaper we read, "A million New Yorkers are good without God. Are you?" This troubled us, not only because of what they said, but more so because we knew that Christians could respond in anger or protest in a manner that would just give us a bad name. We couldn't do that, but what could we do? There were only four of us. But there was something we could do, we could pray. That would be more effective than anything anyone could do.

Someone suggested raising $25,000, just as the atheists did, to put up our own messages showing how necessary God is in the lives of individuals and the city we live in. While it was something that could be done, it didn't seem like it was enough.

Instead I took out my notebook and I jotted down, ***"God Belongs In My City"***. Little did I know this phrase would be the slogan behind a great movement that was completely inspired by God. I knew that the Holy Spirit compelled me to jot down those words. He wanted the team and me to come to a complete understanding that in the midst of the lies the enemy was telling New Yorkers, He belonged there, He dwelled there, and He wanted the body of Christ to come together and proclaim that.

We were a small ministry, with nothing fancy, just four leaders and thirty teens. God began to do amazing things through ordinary people at regular meetings. The key ingredient was faith. We then used the latest technology (Facebook, website, etc.) to share this faith and found others from different churches and denominations who had the same vision to pray together to change our city! God will use regular people in our city and in yours to change our country, one city at a time, through the prayers of His people.

The next idea was to organize a walk where people from Battery Park in lower Manhattan and people coming from the Upper West Side of Manhattan could walk through the streets with T-shirts that said, ***God Belongs In My City***. All participants would meet at Times Square to pray for New York City. While it seemed radical and almost impossible, it was the one idea that sat peacefully in our hearts.

Immediately, I began to call the churches in the Urban Kingdom Youth Ministry Network which I had cofounded. These churches came on board and within days, three hundred individuals mobilized and agreed to take this walk across New York City and proclaim that God belonged there. T-shirts were ordered and plans were made. A video was created using photos of New York City, and a Facebook group page was created. Over the course of the two weeks that followed that initial meeting, T-shirt orders just kept rolling in. Churches were asking for representatives to come speak to their youth and the group page grew to over thirteen hundred members. Three hundred to thirteen hundred, just like that, in only two weeks.

This event just grew! When God births something in the hearts of His children, He takes over and completes His perfect will. Fifteen hundred strong men, women, and children of God knew that He belonged in their city and decided to take a cloudy November morning to proclaim it. Half of the crowd met at Battery Park in Lower Manhattan and the other half met in the Upper West Side of Manhattan. Both groups walked in quiet prayer across Broadway in a sea of white T-shirts with black lettering. With people honking in their cars and trucks, it almost felt like God was cheering us on in a way that kept us aware that He was with us every step of the way. Students were seeing other students from their schools and were hugging each other and forming a bond and a relationship that normally would never have started if it weren't for ***God Belongs In My City***.

After four hours of walking, the two groups finally met at Times Square and walked the red steps of its center. There, all fifteen hundred pairs of hands stretched toward heaven and prayed for God's blessings over New York City. What a profound moment that will forever be etched in the minds and hearts of those who participated—those who were pedestrians on the streets, and onlookers from the buildings, hotels, and high-rises. Tears of joy, tears of realizing how great God truly is, and tears of being in the Almighty God's presence in a place like Times Square began to roll down the cheeks of the crowd. God had come to our city and we were sure of it.

As if that wasn't enough, the army of God walked down to Grand Central Station and in the Great Room, fell to their knees in silent prayer and continued to pray for New York City. What a humbling and sincere moment that changed the lives of everyone there, including a station guard who shared, "Every day I've prayed for this city and the people coming in and out of Grand Central Station. I've asked God for help in praying and today, He's sent me a church to pray with."

This is a movement inspired by God and not by man. It's so important to realize that, because I've found so many individuals approaching me stating that they want to start a movement, and my response is always the same, "You can't start a movement; only God can." The zeal and heart for God is much appreciated and my support will always be there, but honor belongs to whom honor is due. There is no way that on my own strength, or the strength of our team, that we could have organized an event where fifteen hundred people would walk for the cause of Christ. I don't even know fifteen hundred people in New York to be able to mobilize something like that! However, I do know a God who created the heavens and the earth. The same God who told the waters they could only come so far to the shore; the same God who parted the Red Sea; the same God who brought His people out of Egypt; the same God who fed over five thousand people on three fish and two loaves of bread; the same God who sent His son to die for you and me; is the only God who could do this. Because I know and serve the one true God that I am speaking of, He stirred up the hearts of His children to unite and take a stand against the enemy and his plans. He empowered young people to take their schools and cities back for Christ, because He belongs there. What is so beautiful about ***God Belongs In My City*** is that it's not about any one church, any one leader, any specific ministry, or even any particular city. It's about a God who has created and belongs in every single part of this country, the seven continents, the waters, the world, and the universe. We are in desperate need of His hand, His presence, and His mercy, everywhere we go.

We are also in desperate need of each other as we go through this journey of life in Christ. Let's put aside the old and separated ways of doing ministry and join together to be the body of Christ that He calls us to be. The Word of God says:

> [12]Just as a body, though one, has many parts, but all its many parts form one body, so it is with Christ. [13] For we were all baptized by[c] one Spirit so as to form one body—whether Jews or Gentiles, slave or free—and we were all given the one Spirit to drink. [14] Even so the body is not made up of one part but of many.
>
> [15] Now if the foot should say, "Because I am not a hand, I do not belong to the body," it would not for that reason stop being part of the body. [16] And if the ear should say, "Because I am not an eye, I do not belong to the body," it would not for that reason stop being part of the body. [17] If the whole body were an eye, where would the sense of hearing be? If the

whole body were an ear, where would the sense of smell be? [18] But in fact God has placed the parts in the body, every one of them, just as he wanted them to be. [19] If they were all one part, where would the body be? [20] As it is, there are many parts, but one body.

[21] The eye cannot say to the hand, "I don't need you!" And the head cannot say to the feet, "I don't need you!" [22] On the contrary, those parts of the body that seem to be weaker are indispensable, [23] and the parts that we think are less honorable we treat with special honor. And the parts that are unpresentable are treated with special modesty, [24] while our presentable parts need no special treatment. But God has put the body together, giving greater honor to the parts that lacked it, [25] so that there should be no division in the body, but that its parts should have equal concern for each other. [26] If one part suffers, every part suffers with it; if one part is honored, every part rejoices with it.

[27] Now you are the body of Christ, and each one of you is a part of it. (1 Corinthians 12: 12-27)

I am more and more amazed when I read these verses and reflect on ***God Belongs In My City*** because the heart of God is for us to realize that we can't be the world changers like He created us to be on our own. We truly need each other in every sense, and until the body of Christ comes to that realization, we will never be successful in everything He wants us to be. Jesus set such a perfect example when He called on the twelve to be His disciples. He was a perfect man when He walked the earth. He was blameless and came to take the world by storm, but even He brought in Simon (Peter), James, John, Andrew, Philip, Bartholomew, Thomas, Matthew, Thaddaeus, James, Simon, and even Judas, to journey with Him. He saw the importance of other individuals coming alongside Him to help spread the love of His Father. If Jesus included men to walk with Him here on earth, we should also. We can't do this on our own. We need each other. To the leader reading these words and feeling down, know that your answer is a prayer away. You are not alone. There's an army that has gone before you to prepare the way and there's an army now ready to fight and willing to serve with you. Ask God to bring these individuals to light and believe that He will open and close doors to get you where you need to be for His honor and glory.

> Therefore, since we are surrounded by such a great cloud of witnesses, let us throw off everything that hinders and the sin that so easily entangles, and let us run with perseverance the race marked out for us. (Hebrews 12:1)

I'm grateful for the GREAT local leaders and others who have been my partners in ministry, in life, and friendship. Men such as my pastor, Luis Alvarez, Jeremy Del Rio, Larry Acosta, Jacob Burgei, Jack Redmond, Ken Bobe, Waikiki Paulino, Joey Cruz, David Serrano, Chino Arboleda, Adam Durso, Ralph

Castillo, Johnny Lopez, Steve Velez, Chris Durso, Jesus Goyco, Ron Luce, Carlos Beltre, Eddie Zaldana, my three brothers, Jon, Steven, and Timothy, along with their families, and women like Yadira Colon-Lopez, and my incredibly supportive wife, Diane, have journeyed with me. Ken Bobe managed to mobilize four hundred young people from Staten Island alone to participate in the first walk! These men and women have prepared the way and have been by my side in all facets of my ministry and life. They add value to my life and truly make me better. They sharpen me and encourage me to run the race. These individuals are the cream of the crop, and I'm thankful every day that I never feel alone, because I have them in my life.

As one of the cofounders of this event, I am overwhelmed when I think of my team and their obedience to the heart of God. Had they not been sensitive and in tune with the Spirit of God, ***God Belongs In My City*** would never have happened. I feel like a proud father when I think of them and how they allowed the Holy Spirit to birth a true burden for their city and cause them to do something about it. I look at my nephew, Caleb, who was only seven years old at the first walk, and I'm amazed at how every year he tells me how much he loves New York City and how he wants to walk so every New Yorker can know about God. For his eighth birthday, he even asked his mom to organize a New York City-themed party because he wanted him and his friends to wear their ***God Belongs In My City*** T-shirts. God has instilled in him a love for New York City, and I pray that he goes on to do great things for God. It is a true testament to the verse:

> Don't let anyone look down on you because you are young, but set an example for the believers in speech, in life, in love, in faith and in purity. (1Timothy 4:12)

These things are what move me and compel me to strive for unity among the body of Christ. I constantly remind my youth at Crossover Youth Ministry in Brooklyn, New York, to be a Timothy generation and by the grace of God, they strive to be. They often come to me with burdens for their friends, schools, and communities. These students have held on to the heart of God and they want to be the change that they want to see in the world.

Twenty cities and almost two years later, I am still in awe of what God is doing through ***God Belongs In My City***. He is raising an army that is unstoppable! I encourage you all to feel a discontent about the way things are going in your communities and cities all over the world. I encourage you to challenge your leaders and pastors in a respectful way to take back what the devil has stolen! Go out and proclaim that ***God Belongs In My City!***

Chapter 2

You Can Change Your City!

My experience with the God Belongs In My City movement was one that I will never forget. I became aware of the event from the constant traffic of information being posted on Facebook. I was intrigued and asked a good friend what the event was about. Once she told me, I knew I had to be a part of it. I didn't know what I was really getting into, but I woke up early that morning and was ready to walk for a great cause. When I arrived at Battery Park, I was amazed to see so many people from different churches uniting as one. After the opening prayer, I was pumped and ready to tweet every moment—helping to make it a trending topic. Days after my fingers were automatically typing #godbelongsinmycity.

—Rachel-Anne Morales

The problems are too big! There are too many people who are hurting and have too many problems! "Who am I?" "Really?" "What can I do?" "I feel so powerless." Does this sound familiar? You are not alone. People's problems and the problems of our society are overwhelming. They just are. Well, they are to us....

The End of Yourself Brings You to the Beginning of God!

When we get to the end of ourselves, our abilities, our own strength and wisdom, and we lay on our beds totally tired and discouraged, God looks at us and smiles with no sweat and no worries. He knows He is able and ready to help us. But many times we don't turn to Him until we have totally exhausted ourselves or just become discouraged by the inability to change ourselves and the world around us. God's Word teaches us that He is all-powerful, all-knowing, and present everywhere. It also teaches us that He is available and can be known by us. In fact, when we admit we have sinned, that Jesus died on the cross for our sins, and ask Him to forgive us and commit to follow Him, the Holy Spirit actually comes and lives in us and works through us!

> [16] Don't you know that you yourselves are God's temple and that God's Spirit lives in you? (1 Corinthians 3:16)

It's funny how the Apostle Paul is asking this question to the followers of Jesus. Many people who either are or call themselves Christians do not realize that God is available to them in an amazingly real way. So many battles are fought in our own strength and not God's. That's why we struggle so much. Sometimes it's like having Donald Trump for a father and we are trying to survive on some minimum wage job. It's time we fire ourselves and put Jesus in charge of our lives!

> [4]You, dear children, are from God and have overcome them, because the one who is in you is greater than the one who is in the world. (1 John 4:4)

This verse teaches us about spiritual warfare. There are spiritual battles going on all around us. The issues and problems of the world are not just natural problems, they are spiritual. The spiritual problems then become visible and tangible because they eventually cause natural problems. We then try to fight spiritual problems with natural solutions and then become frustrated, because no matter how much we do in the natural, the spiritual problem that causes the natural problems is never dealt with! So even though we help people naturally, the spiritual root keeps producing more natural problems, so the number of problems in society just keeps growing.

We Must Engage in the Spiritual Fight First

> [3]For though we live in the world, we do not wage war as the world does.[4] The weapons we fight with are not the weapons of the world. On the contrary, they have divine power to demolish strongholds. (2 Corinthians 10:3-4)

Strongholds are things that control individuals, families, and even areas of our neighborhoods, cities, and nations. You can't wish them away. They won't go away because you are a nice person. Our fight is first and foremost in the spiritual realm, and it is a fight. Fights are won by the one who is either stronger or who fights better. We have already seen that the Holy Spirit within us is stronger than any other spiritual force, but we must also fight smarter and rely on His strength, guidance, and wisdom.

> [12]For our struggle is not against flesh and blood, but against the rulers, against the authorities, against the powers of this dark world and against the spiritual forces of evil in the heavenly realms. (Ephesians 6:12)

Frustrated in Our Own Ability

People are constantly frustrated by things going on in their neighborhoods, cities, and countries. Everyone is blaming someone else. It's the Republicans; no, it's the Democrats; no, it's the white people; no, it's the black people; no, it's the illegal immigrants. Sound familiar? It's the school system; there's not enough money; it's the teacher's fault; no, it's the parent's; it's the gangs; no, it's the police. It's racism; it's the rich people's fault; no, the poor people are lazy; no, there's no work. The taxes are too high; the rich people don't pay enough taxes; and on and on and on!

You can argue every single point I just made and demonstrate it with some kind of evidence, but where does that get us? If we could change things, we would have already changed them! We need to invite God into the situations and into our cities!

Man's Solutions Don't Work

I often tell people that if they could fix their personal and our societal problems, they would have already done it! The real solutions to the problems in our society are changed hearts and minds. Through our prayers, God moves, changes people, and fixes situations. Demonic strongholds over people, families, neighborhoods, etc., must be broken through prayer. You can build more prisons to lock up criminals, but until the situations, people, and circumstances that help recruit, train, and build criminals are changed, there will be a constant supply of new drug dealers, thieves, and gangbangers.

You can lock up prostitutes, but the pimps will just find more broken and needy young ladies to take their place. You can elect new people, but if their hearts aren't committed to the Lord and strong enough to do what's right, it will just be more of the same. You can lock up gang leaders and members, but until the brokenness of young men is truly dealt with, there will always be new recruits to take the place of those locked up.

Stop Complaining, Stop Being Frustrated, and Ask!

> [2] You want something but don't get it. You kill and covet, but you cannot have what you want. You quarrel and fight. You do not have, because you do not ask God. (James 4:2)

It's amazing how the Bible calls it like it is! Our world is full of people who want good things but don't get them. They desire for the world to change but don't see it. In frustration they fight, argue, want what others have, and some even kill in an effort to get what they want.

We as Christians don't get what we want for one simple reason: we don't ask! So how do we ask? We ask through prayer. ***God Belongs In My City*** is all about teens asking God to bring change and asking for the things that their generation and cities need. We must fight this spiritual battle through prayer. If we ask God, He will supply what we need and change the things that will cause our lives and the lives of our city's people to change.

There is a group of teens from New York City who had enough. They got tired of parts of their city being messed up and decided to do something about it. They didn't try to change the whole world in a day, but they decided to make a change in their city on a November day in 2009. Let's take a walk with our friends who decided that ***God Belongs In My City***.

Taking Action: Take a walk in your town or city and list three things you want to see changed, and then pray about them!

1) ______________________________
2) ______________________________
3) ______________________________

Chapter 3

Prayer, Atheists, and Teens on the Go!

For those who haven't heard the latest news, on November 14, 2009, young people from all over the city motivated their friends and churches for a cause that was more than just another "event." Hearts ran deep with passion to let their voices be known and to declare, "God Belongs In My City." It was a moment in history where young people exercised their right to assembly and their freedom of speech.

—Dorothy Sanabria

Pray for Your City!

Throughout the Bible, God gives us some amazing promises. When we understand that God always keeps His promises, this can be a tremendous encouragement as we go through life.

One of the most commonly quoted Bible verses is Jeremiah 29:11, which clearly tells us that God has created us with great plans and purposes, and it is His will that we succeed, prosper, and that we should have great hope for the future, if we walk in His plans.

> " For I know the plans I have for you," declares the LORD, "plans to prosper you and not to harm you, plans to give you hope and a future. (Jeremiah 29:11)

When people hear this verse, they get excited! In their minds, it's just going to happen. If it's God's will, He will make it happen. First thing is that God's Word is His will. It is His plan. His will and our choice are two separate things. The reality is that He gives us free will. We can choose His will or create our own. We must also line up our lives with His ways to live His will. If we are not willing to do that, we will just have to take what life hands us!

God's Promises Are Often Conditional

People often want God's promises to come to pass, but the reality is that if God's promises are to be fulfilled, it requires certain actions and attitudes on our behalf. God works on principles and order, and one of the greatest things we must do if we want to see our cities prosper is to pray for the peace and prosperity of our cities. Let's go back a few verses to help us understand the setting of God's promise in Jeremiah 29:11.

> [7] Also, seek the peace and prosperity of the city to which I have carried you into exile. Pray to the LORD for it, because if it prospers, you too will prosper. (Jeremiah 29:7)

As God's people pray, work, and seek for the peace and prosperity of their city, the spiritual atmosphere changes. God's presence brings peace and power. Many Christians are upset about their personal lives. They don't like the school they are in or there's too much violence and drugs on the streets. Too many people are being chewed up and spit out by gangs, jails, and the sexual culture that is destroying so many minds, spirits, and bodies. We see so much destruction on the daily news, and these things are not God's will for the lives of the people being hurt. We must pray for the peace and prosperity of our city.

But You Don't Know About MY City!

True, I don't know everything that has gone on in your city, but God does. People often read Jeremiah 29:11 by itself and get all excited about God's great plans and purposes, but they don't know to whom and where this promise is being told.

Jeremiah 29:11 Was Spoken to a Conquered and Broken People

Due to the Israelite's rebellion, God allowed them to be conquered and taken into captivity into Babylon, which is in modern-day Iraq. So God's people chose to rebel, were conquered, and taken into captivity from Israel and were now in Babylon. When God was telling the Israelites to pray for the peace and prosperity of the city of Babylon, the Israelites were being told to pray for the success of their conquerors! God said that if the Babylonians prospered, so would the Israelites.

So if God told His people to pray for the peace and prosperity of the people in that city, how much more should we pray for ours? God promised to later take them out of captivity and bring them back to Israel, and He did. But in the meantime, God told them to live their lives in this tough situation until that time came.

Much of our cities have been conquered by sin, overwhelming needs, and the inability of man to deal with the issues and problems of people. People flock to cities because of the opportunities and communities needed to live, but along with these benefits, there also can be many struggles and problems.

Cities = Lots of People and Lots of Problems

The reality is that our cities are filled with thousands—if not millions—of people. Everyone has problems, so the more people, the more problems. It's simple math! This is why we need God's intervention in individuals' lives first, then into the schools, businesses, and governments these people make up. God changes cities if His people pray. The question is, will you pray?

Many people have been conquered by poverty, sin, greed, or injustice. Our cities are filled with people who are controlled by these things. These issues drive some people straight to God. They drive many other people away from God. We spend our time sharing the hope and love of God with teens, but others in our city are convinced that with all of these problems, there can't be a God.

We agree on one thing: things must change. The question is how?

Atheist Billboards—One Million Are Good Without God. Are you?

It was Monday morning, November 2, 2009, and it was my birthday (Danny). Someone put an article on the desk about an atheist billboard campaign that said:

"One million New Yorkers are good without God. Are you?" To let atheists know that they were not alone. Emotions flooded the room. Some felt anger that people would so boldly and publicly reject God and encourage others to do so. Others felt sorrow for people who have been turned off by religion and hurt by the acts of men. Hurt even to the point that they would reject God because they don't understand how much God loves and wants to help them.

As we worked through the emotions, we knew that we needed to do something and the question was put forth: "What are we going to do about this?" I (Danny) wrote down the words, ***"God Belongs In My City"*** in a notebook, and we started to get the ball rolling. Someone suggested, "What if we get T-shirts and walk the streets?" Another added, "Let's not protest this; let the T-shirts be the message." Someone else chimed in, "Let's do a prayer walk." ***God Belongs In My City*** **(GBIMC)** was born on a Monday morning at a youth leader meeting.

Planning the Prayer Walk

At this point we were focused on having a prayer walk. We began to dream. "Let's call all the leaders of the Urban Kingdom Youth Network," someone said. We thought, "Imagine if we could get three hundred teens!" Little did we know or even expect that God was about to blow our minds! We knew the weather was getting colder and decided we should do the prayer walk within the next two weeks before the temperature really dropped.

I (Danny) started calling youth pastors. Our young adult small group was on board. We had a website the next day, www.Godbelongsinmycity.com, and a Facebook group page. We had no money, no backing by any organization, just a dream.

Ordering 300 T-shirts with No Money!

By faith we ordered three hundred T-shirts without realizing that we needed to actually pay for them when we picked them up! We called our T-shirt printer and he said he would deliver them without payment. We were able to sell them and quickly ordered three hundred more. We kept selling and ordering T-shirts until we realized that we sold two thousand T-shirts in just two weeks!

The Youth Started Taking Over!

The teens started to spread the word and before we knew it, the teens were telling their youth pastors about ***GBIMC*** instead of the pastors trying to get the kids to go! The youth wanted to pray for their city. They wanted to express loud and clear that New York City was not fine and that their city needed God! They love their city. New York is one of the greatest cities on the planet, but without Jesus, people and the city will continue to experience the same problems. When we get to the real issue, crime, sin, and problems always begin with people's hearts and actions.

Atheists Were Willing to Invest $25,000 for Their Cause

The reality that people would invest $25,000 of their own hard-earned money to promote believing in nothing is a sign of the level of sin sickness that has overtaken our country and culture. You cannot embrace atheism unless you have been repeatedly bombarded with anti-God messages while simultaneously walking in the pain caused by the sin that is all around us each day. It is understandable how people get there, but it is a wrong and hopeless conclusion.

All People Must Establish a Spiritual Reality

Every person on the planet must come to some type of conclusion about a spiritual reality. That's why people and groups in every society throughout history have developed some type of religious, philosophical, or spiritual belief system. This system sets the moral code, philosophy, and religious practices for individuals and groups of people. One of the conclusions that people can come to is that there is no God. This can only happen when a person rejects the different religious choices they have been presented with.

So what are atheists left with? When people have tried the different things that our world offers and find out that nothing satisfies their deepest and strongest needs, a frustration sets in. Since "everything" they have experienced doesn't fulfill, atheists stop trying to believe in God and begin to put their faith in natural things like knowledge, experience, etc. From a spiritual sense, they disengage and put their faith in the belief that God doesn't exist, and they stop pursuing a God they feel is not real. The next level is often becoming angry that people are putting their faith in "nothing" or some type of fairy tale, since they believe God doesn't exist. They then become the very thing they are fighting against and purposely put their faith in "nothing," which they call atheism—the concept that God does not exist. They can then intellectually fight to promote their personal faith in a godless existence and promote the passionate belief in "no God."

Passion for "Nothing"

It is amazing how people can have so much passion and desire to believe in nothing. They are driven to prove that life has no Creator, no purpose, and therefore no real meaning outside of what they make. While I can understand that many have been disillusioned by what some have done through organized religion and the actions of people, there is a huge difference between what broken people have done and the atheists' conclusion that God doesn't exist because of the shortcomings of people.

At the end of the day, when atheists fight with all of their might against having faith, they are actually just creating another faith. They build a belief system of their own, placing knowledge, experience, or themselves as supreme. Atheism has defined beliefs and actions in the same way that all religions do, and in fact, atheism itself requires a very strong faith that there is no God or even a possibility of God.

Many atheists are genuinely concerned people who are intellectually honest and have concluded from their life experience and investigation that there is no God. The issue is that sincerity and truth can be two different things.

People Can Be Sincerely Wrong!

The world is full of people who have deep convictions and are sincere but are wrong. Some beliefs are wrong but harmless. How many people have really believed that the next experience, the next relationship, the next job, will really make them happy, but it doesn't. There are times when life experience teaches us that even in our sincerity, we can be wrong.

For years, well-meaning doctors used leeches to remove people's blood because they thought that sickness was in the blood, and if you removed enough blood, you would take away the sickness. Researchers have found skulls of people that doctor's drilled holes through to relieve headaches. Others thought the world was flat, while many thought it was round. Columbus thought that he landed in India because he had no reason to think there were entire continents between Europe and Asia. All these people meant well, but because of their lack of knowledge, they were sincere, but wrong, in their thoughts or actions. All of these people were also trying to do great things that would help people.

Other examples include people who have fought and died for wrong beliefs. People like Adolph Hitler were sincere but terribly misguided in their passions and convictions, and millions paid for it.

While I don't think that the average atheist is physically dangerous in any way, their belief system is eternally dangerous to themselves and others. In fact, I would go as far as to say that most atheists feel they are good people and are doing good things by helping others leave or not get involved in a "false religion" or a God that in their minds doesn't exist. There are also many atheists who have done many good things and contributed in many positive ways to our society. They can also point to many religious people throughout history that have hurt, oppressed, and killed people from many different faith systems in an attempt to advance their beliefs.

Religion (man's efforts to reach and represent God) always falls short of the wonderful loving God of the Bible! It is the very fallen nature and inability of man that causes us to need a savior and to "be saved!" This savior is Jesus of Nazareth, God in flesh, and the only hope of mankind!

Taking Action: Create a list of reasons why you follow Jesus and what He has done in your life to share with someone.

Reasons I believe what I believe about Jesus:

1) ______________________________
2) ______________________________
3) ______________________________
4) ______________________________

I will share these with: ______________________________

____

Always be prepared to give an answer to everyone who asks you to give the reason for the hope that you have. But do this with gentleness and respect. (1 Peter 3:15)

Chapter 4

Healing Our Land Through the Power of Prayer

Perhaps the most moving experience of the walk was the final prayer, where a group of well over five hundred people got on their knees in the middle of Grand Central Station, unified in prayer. It was such an amazing way to conclude such a memorable day, to make a public declaration of our faith. Interestingly enough, when you hear that someone is participating in a walk, you can draw many negative conclusions. Nevertheless, that did not seem to be the case here. Despite the events that led up to the day, our group did not run out looking to challenge or protest, but to simply declare that God Belongs In Our City.

—Eden Martinez, Abounding Grace Ministries

Don't Let What People Do Get in the Way of What God Wants to Do!

In speaking with people who are struggling with the concept of God, I (Jack) have often asked them to tell me what they have against God, and it becomes clear very quickly that their issues and problems are not with God, but with what people have done. We will look more into this later, but let's grow in our understanding that God wants to change and heal our land.

Healing Our Sin Sick Land

> [14] If my people, who are called by my name, will humble themselves and pray and seek my face and turn from their wicked ways, then will I hear from heaven and will forgive their sin and will heal their land. [15] Now my eyes will be open and my ears attentive to the prayers offered in this place. (2 Chronicles 7:14-15)

Humbling ourselves is often accompanied by outward deliberate actions such as times of prayer and fasting. Humbling ourselves means purposely demonstrating, privately or publicly, that we don't know it all and we don't have control over everything. It shows that we need God and are willing to do what we need to do to open ourselves to His will and His ways. Humility gets God's attention. It often is accompanied by action or change in how we do things. In this Scripture, turning from their wicked ways is part of the conditions to having their prayer answered.

Sin—The Root of Every Problem!

I want to talk about sin because it is the root of all man's problems. Sin causes spiritual death and separation from God. It also systematically destroys a person emotionally, spiritually, and physically. It is not just a religious issue that someone standing in the front of the church is yelling about. Sin is real and so are its consequences. Our culture and society both deny sin and promote it. Our society often acts like sin is not harmful in any way and does everything it can to get teens to buy into a self-destructive lifestyle. After the sin sickness takes hold of people, they understand it in a different way, but many times don't know how to escape from its grip.

Defining Sin

In its simplest definition, sin is anything that is different or outside the will, plans, and ways of God. God created us to live great lives that are dominated and filled with love, purpose, and great experiences. The hate, wasted lives, and devastation we see on a daily basis are the result of sin and are outside of God's will for our lives. They are the result of living without God and then often used to dispute the goodness or very existence of Him! We are at times also the recipients and victims of other people's sin.

Understanding the Devastation of Sin

Sin separates us from both God and people. It is offensive to God and hurts those around us and ourselves. The reason many people become atheists is because they see the devastation of sin in crimes and come to the conclusion that there is either no God, He is unable to stop evil, or they think that God is the cause of everything. They want nothing to do with a God that is unable to stop or would cause the chaos and pain that surrounds us. These are reasonable conclusions if you start with the wrong ideas. God is trying to get us through and away from the pain and senselessness of so many things. Because of their pain and what they have seen, atheists are actually denying the only thing that can help them!

Why Does God Allow Sin?

God gave us free will because He did not want us to be robots. He created us to have a relationship with Him, and you can only have a relationship if you choose to! He not only wants us to choose Him, but to also choose His ways. We can't really choose Him and His ways unless we have the freedom to reject Him and His ways! We can't choose right unless we choose it over wrong. When we choose wrong, we sin and cause pain and destruction to ourselves and others. Even if it is not immediate, sin eventually destroys people, relationships, and families. It can keep growing until it affects all areas of our society. The question is: "Are we just going to sit around and suffer the consequences of individual and societal sin, or do something about it?"

Taking Ownership of YOUR Generation

These teens took a huge step that day toward taking ownership for the spiritual condition of their generation! God has called you to be salt and light! (Matthew 5:13-16) Our culture has been overrun with concepts that it is someone else's job to change things or that things will get better by themselves. Or even more often, nobody thinks they actually can change things, so why bother! But not the teens of New York City! They had enough and decided they want change and that change can only come when people invite God into the situation to bring the transforming power and healing that only He can bring!

Called by My Name

People who have chosen to be called by God's name have access to Him in ways that others don't. These teens who have committed their lives to serve Jesus as their Lord and Savior decided to not let these blessings and power just sit on a shelf, but decided to use it! They decided to represent the One they love.

Praying for Your City in Your City

When our teens prayed, they knew that they would be heard because of this promise in God's Word:

> [15] Now my eyes will be open and my ears attentive to the prayers offered in this place. (2 Chronicles 7:15)

This was a promise from God to Solomon after the temple had been finished. God appeared to Solomon and declared that prayers said at this place would be heard and answered in a way that would bless the land! In the new covenant of Jesus, the situation is even better!

> [19] Do you not know that your body is a temple of the Holy Spirit, who is in you, whom you have received from God? (1 Corinthians 6:19)

For the Jewish people, the temple was the place where they sought God and was God's dwelling place. These teens knew that when they received Jesus as Lord and Savior, they received the Holy Spirit, who now literally makes residence within them! Filled with the Holy Spirit and God's power, they prayed on the streets of New York City and then in Grand Central Station, which is the hub of public transportation in the most influential city on the planet! Nameless multitudes of teens, filled with God's power, humbled themselves and prayed that God would change people's lives and heal their city.

God Belongs In My City—November 14, 2009

Our dream was to have three hundred teens pray for New York City, and God blew our minds that day! We never expected such an explosion of teens. This day was a deliberate day when fifteen hundred teens publicly displayed their humility and asked their Lord to heal their land! This act was not done to bring any publicity to a person, but to declare their need and their city's need for Jesus. It was a demonstration of His Lordship over teens, adults, and New York City as a whole!

Taking Action: Stand in the gap and pray for your generation!!! Three things (sins) I will repent for on behalf of my generation and pray that God heals the damage caused by them:

1) ____
2) ____
3) ____

Chapter 5

Passion, Four Youth Leaders, and a Notebook

We continued the Monday morning meeting attempting to plan out our week, but couldn't stop talking about this atheist campaign. But what could we do as a small youth ministry in Brooklyn? We needed to make a statement, something people could remember, but also something that wasn't loud and obnoxious. The advertisement said, "A million New Yorkers are good without God. Are you?"

The problem was that a million New Yorkers were without God and, as a Christian, this was a sad realization. Many in this city are without God. Something needed to change, and that something was up to us. We needed to pray for our city, and we needed the people to know that God belonged here in this city, and that we Christians were the agents of change that God would use to announce it.

—Noel Soto, Park Slope Christian Tabernacle

So armed with our notebook with the five words, ***"God Belongs In My City"*** scribbled on it, we began a journey. We were then armed with fifteen hundred teens wearing ***God Belongs In My City*** T-shirts who were filled God's Holy Spirit and a desire to see lives and communities transformed through the power of prayer.

Our teens were tired of being defined by the media and being pushed aside as powerless and irrelevant by so many in our society. Our youth were determined to make a difference this day and every day by their actions and prayers!

You could feel the passion and enthusiasm as fifteen hundred teens embraced being world changers on that cold November morning. No big names, no celebrities, the only one we wanted to make famous on this day was Jesus! And Jesus does miracles every day through people who embrace the call.

Salt and Light

> [13]You are the salt of the earth. But if the salt loses its saltiness, how can it be made salty again? It is no longer good for anything, except to be thrown out and trampled by men.
>
> [14] You are the light of the world. A city on a hill cannot be hidden. [15]Neither do people light a lamp and put it under a bowl. Instead they put it on its stand,

and it gives light to everyone in the house. [16] In the same way, let your light shine before men, that they may see your good deeds and praise your Father in heaven. (Matthew 5:13-16)

In a world where so many struggle to define themselves or understand what their purpose is, Jesus clearly defines who and what His followers are and what they are supposed to do. They are to be salt and light!

Salt does three things:

1) It preserves the good that exists in a food.
2) It prevents bacteria from causing decay and spoilage.
3) Salt brings out the flavor—it makes things better.

So Jesus is defining what it means to be a Christ follower. We are to preserve the best of society, prevent moral, spiritual, and social decay, and enhance the good that is already there!

So what about light? Light does some interesting things also:

1) It lets you see what is really there and things as they really are!
2) It lights up the dark areas where it shines.
3) In the Bible, the word light can also mean "truth" or "good deeds," which are evidence of God working in your life.

Jesus is telling His followers to shine a light on His truth and to help people really see things as they actually are. This drives people to God as they see that without Him, there is no hope. Atheists have come to the conclusion of the hopelessness of man and then assigned this hopelessness to God. They then reject the hope of God and put their faith and hope in man! Talk about getting things twisted.

A Shining Light or Something That Needs to Be Flushed?

Jesus said that salt that lost its saltiness wasn't worth anything and needed to be thrown in the manure pile. A manure pile, for all the city folks, is a big pile of animal poop. Does your life resemble a shining bright light that points people to Jesus, or something that should be flushed down the toilet? To qualify for the toilet, your life doesn't have to really stink; it just needs to have no spiritual power or fruit. No power + no fruit = FLUSH.

The Atheists Have a Point

Jesus and the atheists agree on at least one thing. A faith that has no power and brings no positive change is worthless! I (Jack) have had many conversations over the years with people who are wrestling with the whole concept of God or who have chosen to reject God as nonsense that men have made up. The conversation usually follows a pretty similar path. I ask them why they believe and feel the way that they do, and they usually become somewhat emotional and passionate as they talk about their issues.

Is the Problem God or Man?

As they begin to crank out a laundry list of issues and complaints, they are usually very surprised that I agree with most of what they say. Then, I usually ask them one question: "Did God do that or man?" Common issues or questions include things like:

1) Millions of people have been killed because of "religion."
2) Religion doesn't change people.
3) I used to go to church, but nothing changed.
4) If there is a God, why are so many things messed up?

I could go on and on, but just a couple of things that people bring up. First, people have done all kinds of horrible things, but at the end of the day, they are choices and actions of people. God has given man free will and the ability to choose. We can choose a relationship with Him or reject it. We can choose His ways or reject them. We can only know His ways when we know Him!

If you have been a church attendee but have not experienced any change, that's a problem! Let me tell you one thing I've learned: when there is a problem and I have to figure out if the problem is me or God, it has always been me! But He still loves me and patiently walks with me as I grow and He changes me.

Created for Relationship

Religion is man's attempt to reach God, but we cannot do that in our own strength. Religion always hits a dead end because it depends on man's efforts and abilities. I often say that when we come to the end of ourselves we have only gotten to the beginning of God! Jesus came to reach us! He removed the barrier of sin. All of man's religious efforts around the world, no matter what it's called, are futile attempts to connect with a God who can only be connected through His grace and the cross. Religion doesn't change people; only a relationship with the living God does that. While going to a Bible-believing and teaching church is crucial to spiritual growth, there are billions of people going to churches, temples, and mosques in an effort to please a distant God. Though these efforts are often noble and sincere, it is only faith in the work of the cross that truly connects us with God. It is then that we can follow Jesus into His plans and purposes as we walk in His power! But this is a personal choice and lifestyle.

It's All About Free Will

Free will is the ability to make choices and decisions on our own. Because of free will, we can accept or reject God. We can choose right or wrong. We can embrace truth or something else. It is the compounded choices of men over the ages that created the society that we live in. We have the choice to love or hate, to bless or curse. God has told us His will in His Word. It is the ignorance or rejection of His Word that causes the problems that result in people blaming or rejecting God.

Many people have also had powerless of even bad church experiences and decided to stop seeking God. Let's live each day and be salt and light as we share the love of Christ with our friends, classmates, and everyone we know. People don't need a dead church experience; they need to connect to the living God, and that happens most often through His spiritually alive children.

Taking Action: Create an Atheist Prayer List!!! List people you know who claim to be atheists and begin to pray and work to lead them to Jesus!

1) ____
2) ____
3) ____

> Therefore, I urge you, brothers, in view of God's mercy, to offer your bodies as living sacrifices, holy and pleasing to God—this is your spiritual act of worship. (Romans 12:1)

Jesus died so that we could live. We should live to help others live in Jesus!

Chapter 6

The Body of Christ Rising Up

During the Monday morning youth meeting, I saw the newspaper with the atheist ad on the cover, and I read that they where placing the ad all over New York City—on the buses, and even the trains. I was crushed by the fact that they where saying that my God was a meaningless, nonexistent fairy tale of a God, and even worse, I knew that the "Christians" were not going to do anything about it. And if they did take action, it would be one of those hyper, overly loud protests that, in my opinion, are what is giving Christendom a bad name.

—Noel Soto, Park Slope Christian Tabernacle

The passive church is a dying church. Statistically, many churches are stagnant or decreasing in size. Many youth are leaving church because they are bored out of their minds, and the reality for many is that attending church doesn't really impact their lives in a meaningful way. There is also no demand placed on them. Most pastors and parents are happy if they can just get teens to show up and are afraid to ask them for anything else because they fear this will "drive them away from God." The reality is that "anyone" who is not doing anything for God on some level is already "away from God." You can't really claim to love God if you are not doing His will and His works!

> [46] Why do you call me, 'Lord, Lord,' and do not do what I say? (Luke 6:46)

> So when you give...; (Matthew 6:2) And when you pray...; (Matthew 6:5) ...When you fast.... (Matthew 6:16)

Teens Are Wired to Live on the Edge

Since the beginning of time, teenage and young adult years have been a time of action and adventure. God has placed a natural curiosity and need for adventure within us. One of the greatest problems in youth ministry today is that we don't ask or offer adventure or challenge our teens. We offer a place to sit, songs and words to listen to, but no adventure beyond that! We wanted our youth to take a stand. For generations, adults have fought for the youth. It is time for the youth to fight for their own generation! We decided to not just call youth leaders, but to put a demand on teens to take ownership for their generation and for our culture. Teens both set culture and are used by others to set culture for them. It is time for our teens to be used by God to establish His will and purpose in their city!

We Sounded the Trumpet

Throughout the Old Testament, the people of God sounded the trumpet at times to gather the people to either seek God or to proceed in war. We began to sound the trumpet to gather followers of Christ to go to war in prayer for the city of New York. The trumpet was the highest technology in those days to communicate a clear message over long distances, but we have a few more advanced forms of communication these days!

We Blew the Internet Trumpet!

The trumpets of this youth generation are much different. Their trumpets are e-mails, Facebook posts and YouTube clips! As Joshua's trumpet blast called the twelve tribes of Israel to shout, we started calling different youth pastors and churches for a sacred time of prayer for our city through our network, and the message began to spread. We had two weeks to gather hundreds of teens to pray for our city. There was not a lot of time, but the passion was burning and we had to do something about it.

The response was amazing! Many people would think that teens would not be passionate about prayer, but we found out something much different. There are many teens who want to see change in their cities and in their generation. This became clear as the teens began to take charge and reach out to their friends.

We began by calling youth pastors we know, and it began to build like a snowball rolling downhill. We started the ball rolling, but soon it was rolling on its own. The buzz began to grow as people sent e-mails and Facebook invites. Teens started pressuring their youth pastors to go to ***GBIMC*** instead of youth pastors trying to drag teens to some event. The spirit of unity and excitement became contagious and spread on its own. We began to realize that God was doing something bigger than we ever imagined. In twelve days, without any budget or advertising, we went from a room with four people to over fifteen hundred strong taking to the streets in New York City! God is amazing!

Taking Action: Living on the edge!!! Don't wait for the world to change—go change it!

If you could do anything in your church or in your schools for Jesus, what would it be?

____

____

____

____

____

____

____

Chapter 7

Empowering Young People—The Church of Today!

God Belongs In My City marked an epic visual representation of what a body united can say. Initially, I didn't really know what to expect. Sometimes my idea of a church gathering is quite limited in expectation, but mostly in numbers. As I arrived at the Battery Park meet-up, I quickly realized this was not simply another church gathering. Making my way through the crowd, I saw youth boldly standing up for their beliefs and ready to represent God in an open forum. This was a sense of representation that in youth culture I felt had definitely been lost; however, I soon realized it had simply been misplaced. Being a leader, it definitely made me consider whether or not I had been working to create forums such as this, where youth are given an opportunity to stand up for what they believed in. Needless to say, I could not seem to shake the excitement.

—Eden Martinez, Abounding Grace Ministries

Too many times I have heard children and teens referred to as "The Church of Tomorrow" by the adult generation. While this has a level of truth in it, that they will lead our churches in the future, too often this mentality puts our teens in a box of uselessness until they grow up. There is nowhere in the Bible that puts an age limit on being used by God. There are guidelines of character and maturity when dealing with putting people in authority over God's people, but that is different than someone being used by God to pray or lead people to Christ and serve people in a powerful way!

> [12] Don't let anyone look down on you because you are young, but set an example for the believers in speech, in life, in love, in faith and in purity. (1 Timothy 4:12)

It's funny how many in the church do the exact opposite of this Scripture. First they treat youth like they are powerless in God's Kingdom; and secondly, they don't expect them to live in purity and have strong faith. We need to train our youth to live lives of faith, love, and purity in thought, word, and action, and not treat them like they are useless until they become adults.

Youth Are the Greatest Mission Field on the Planet

In America and around the world, teens and young adults are key in shaping our world and fulfilling the Great Commission. In some countries, half the population is under twenty-five years old. Many of these countries have no organized focus on reaching youth. We need to have many strong adults who are focused on winning this generation to Christ, but the greatest mission team available is teens going after their friends.

I (Jack) have grown to see youth as a separate "people group" in our society. What differentiates cultures are things like language, communication, clothes, and behavior. This youth generation clearly has a different language, communication system, and acts differently than previous generations. We often spend so much time trying to train older generations to connect to youth instead of teaching youth how to share God's Word in the language that already comes natural to them.

In a mission field there are often barriers to cross-cultural ministries such as language, culture, and communication. The most effective missionaries are often indigenous people who have been trained in the Gospel but who then are able to communicate in a common language. Teens are already equipped to reach other teens!

Having Vision to Change YOUR Generation

One of the most exciting things that happens as you walk with Jesus is that He begins to help you see things the way He sees them and the way that He wants them! He then helps you order your life so that you can live out His dreams!

> [18]Where there is no revelation, the people cast off restraint; (Proverbs 29:18a)

Revelation is the process where God reveals the vision and plans He has for you, your generation, and the world! Many teens are scared of the world they are growing up in because of what they see. The reality is that many of the things that are going on are not God's will but the result of the choices and actions of people. When you seek God and His will, He will begin to show you a better reality. If you can envision a better society, God will use you to make it happen!

God Brings Order Out of Disorder

Restraint means limitation. When we have goals and dreams, we have the motivation to order our lives differently so that we can live our dreams instead of just thinking about them! It's funny how it is only through purposely limiting ourselves that we can achieve the limitless dreams of God! This type of limitation isn't designed to hold us captive, but to set us free to focus our time and energy on greater things that we can't achieve without these imposed limitations.

It is kind of like playing a basketball game. You have to show up at a certain time, stay inside the lines of the court, and follow a list of rules if you want to play and win. These limitations create focused individuals and groups of people to complete a task.

If an individual or team refuses to follow the rules, they will lose or not even be able to play the game. In life, we have to live certain ways to get the results we want. We can only win in life when we order (restrict) our lives to live in a way to win our battles and overcome our challenges.

Millions of teens order their lives and restrict their actions to play sports, join clubs, or to be musicians, dancers, actors, and to get good grades. While these are all good, God wants us to order our spiritual lives and priorities too! God not only wants us to order our individual lives, but He also puts us together with others for greater purposes than we could achieve on our own!

But I Can't Do It All by Myself!

Exactly, and you're not meant to! God's Word teaches you that you are one piece of an entire body. You don't have to do everything! You just have to do your part!

> [12] The body is a unit, though it is made up of many parts; and though all its parts are many, they form one body. So it is with Christ. (1 Corinthians 12:12)

Don't Let What You Can't Do Get in the Way of What You Can Do!

People of all ages wrestle with feeling insignificant in such a big world. Many want to change the world but feel as if their own "small" effort won't make a difference. The reality is that the world is seldom changed by one person who does one thing. The world is most often changed slowly over time by the cumulative effects of small actions of millions of people over time. The reality is that if everyone smiled and said, "thank you," all the time, our world would be changed! How much more if an entire generation began to pray and the power of God began to radically change one person, one school, and one city at a time? The key is not trying to do it all by yourself, but to do what God is calling you to do where you live, work, and play each day!

> [26]If one part suffers, every part suffers with it; if one part is honored, every part rejoices with it. (1 Corinthians 12:26)

This verse lets us know that we don't have to seek honor because serving God is a team game! If one part is honored, every part rejoices. It's like winning a Super Bowl. It is better to be a role-player or backup on the championship team than to be the star of a losing team! The body also suffers when you suffer. If the body of Christ is weak, those that belong to it also suffer and society as a whole then suffers! Many people have had weak church experiences because many within the body didn't do their part. You can't make everyone do what God has called them to do, but you can step up and do and be all God has called you to do and be!

Many Are Looking for Encouragement

It's been said that 98 percent of all people are followers and only about 2 percent are leaders. Our world is full of people who will do things if someone else leads! You don't have to be a "leader" to lead. Leading people just means influencing them to do something. What we do each day influences people in the way they speak, dress, act, what they watch on TV, look at on the computer, etc. We are all influencers in getting people to do what we do and like what we like.

When we step up and publicly pray, others will follow. When you stand up for Jesus, you are paving the road for others to travel. If you lead one other person, you have doubled your impact! If you lead ten other people, your influence has multiplied ten times what you could do on your own. That doesn't even count the people they will begin to lead and influence to do God's will! Jesus focused on changing twelve and changed the world! We just have to start seeing beyond the realities of our world and our personal limitations and start to see what God sees and wants to do!

You Have to See a Better Reality

> [18] Where there is no revelation, the people cast off restraint. (Proverbs 29:18a)

Our society can be defined by this one verse of Scripture. When people live without the revealed will of God in their lives, they live unrestrained lives. "Friends with benefits," rampant pornography, all kinds of drug and alcohol use, are all the results of people living a life without God's vision for their lives. It results in living and doing anything for a quick thrill or doing things just because they have no sense of the long-term results.

But when someone can see a better society caused by better lives, they will order their lives to be and bring the change that they see. If you can see that God belongs in your city, you will begin to live and pray in a way that invites and establishes His presence in a greater way. You will begin to represent Him in your classrooms and the hallway of your schools. You will bring His presence with you into the locker room and onto the streets each and every day.

Relationships Get Results

It is only through a growing passionate relationship with Jesus that you will continually be led to do His will. It is only through relationship that you will see the transforming power of Jesus Christ in your life. When you continually grow and change to live your purpose and to become more like Jesus, it is only natural that you will love and serve more and more just like Jesus.

The next step is then to desire to see the same type of changes in other people's lives. You can't just sit around and watch people live meaningless and painful lives with no hope. You can't watch injustice and people struggle and suffer and do nothing about it! ***God Belongs In My City*** has grown because teens around the country have said: "Enough is enough! I want my voice to be heard!" The reality is that your voice may never be heard in a significant way by people in your city, but it can be heard by the One who created the whole world and has the power to bring change when we pray!

> [12] I tell you the truth, anyone who has faith in me will do what I have been doing. He will do even greater things than these, because I am going to the Father. [13] And I will do whatever you ask in my name, so that the Son may bring glory to the Father. [14] You may ask me for anything in my name, and I will do it. (John 14:12-14)

Anyone Means Anyone—And That Means YOU!

We need you to get a hold of this fact. ANYONE who has a real-deal faith in Jesus can do what He did! Real faith means real power. Wherever Jesus went, things changed when He prayed. When you pray, God hears and it moves Him to action. When we ask for things that line up with God's will, He does them! You have the ability to pray in agreement with God's Word and He will do it!

> [14] "This is the confidence we have in approaching God: that if we ask anything according to his will, he hears us. (1 John 5:14)

When you go out and pray, you can have a ridiculous amount of confidence! Dig into God's Word because God's

Word is God's will! If we use the principles and actual words of God found in the Bible and pray them in faith, we can be sure that God is going to get involved in our lives and in our cities! As we pray for our cities to match up and reflect cities that honor God, we should expect change.

You Don't Have to Vote to Bring Change!

While I do encourage you to be educated and involved in the political process, you don't have to be able to vote to influence your city! In fact, your prayers have more power than a single vote! Also like voting, when you pray, the more people that you have who join and agree with you, the more power you will have! It is great when one person prays; there is more power when two or three agree and pray; and as the number increases, so does the power!

> [18]I tell you the truth, whatever you bind on earth will be bound in heaven, and whatever you loose on earth will be loosed in heaven.
> [19]Again, I tell you that if two of you on earth agree about anything you ask for, it will be done for you by my Father in heaven. [20]For where two or three come together in my name, there am I with them. (Matthew 18:18-20)

There are also things in our society that will not change without prayer! There are heavenly powers and principalities that must be broken before we see certain changes. When we join in agreement with others and pray according to God's will, it brings God's presence and power in a greater way. We don't always know the results of our prayers because they are sometimes answered immediately; other times a change process is started; and other times it may take time before we see the victory of our prayers.

Praying As a Lifestyle

Our prayers should be part of our lifestyle, not just an occasional activity.

> [16]Be joyful always; [17]pray continually; (1 Thessalonians 5:16-17)

Other translations say pray "without ceasing," which lets us know that we should be praying continually. While we should get together for a specific time and events like ***GBIMC***, we should also pray as we go about our daily business in school, in the neighborhood, etc.

I Have Seen Prayer Work!

When I was a new youth leader (Jack), I remember seeing teens in Krauszer's or CVS and my heart would just break. I would pray that they would be saved in the store but not talk to them because I didn't know them or have an opportunity to. A few weeks would go by and I would be preaching at Teen Church. I would give an altar call for people to receive Jesus or ask people to come up to receive prayer about a certain issue. Time after time, I would see that teen I saw buying gum or chips at the store a few weeks ago. But now they were in my church, in our youth service, and crying at the altar because Jesus touched them. I just did what Jesus put on my heart and He did the rest. God will use you in the same way. Let His heart be your heart and His power will work through you!

Praying Together Is Even More Powerful Than Praying Alone!

God teaches us to get together to pray. If God says that He is with us when two or three get together, He is in the midst. You can only imagine the presence of God we felt at Grand Central Station when over five hundred youth and adults knelt down and prayed for God to change and bless our city!

Taking Action: Get a prayer and action partner and focus on praying for different people to connect them to Jesus and help them along the way and after. Make a list of people from all walks of life that you want to see impacted by Jesus:

1) Honor Roll Student ______________________
2) Dropout ______________________
3) Jock ______________________
4) Rocker ______________________
5) Hip-Hopper ______________________
6) Skater ______________________
7) Homey ______________________

8) Immigrant ______________________________

9) Rich ______________________________

10) Poor ______________________________

Others… ______________________________

Chapter 8

Encountering New York City

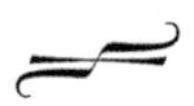

As we walked through the streets and passed the sights and crowds of Manhattan, the excitement only seemed to build. Truthfully, I have never updated my Twitter and Facebook status so much in one day in order to keep constant track of every move we made. At one point, a friend became slightly overwhelmed with memories as we walked past the World Trade Center site. I thought it only fitting, and somewhat ironic, that a body of believers was walking past this site and expressing an equally overwhelming emotion of our love for Christ.

—Eden Martínez, Abounding Grace Ministries

Teens mold and shape culture today in stronger ways than at any other time in history! Throughout history, culture has been driven by adults. In former times, youth did not have the ability to significantly shape culture, but this has changed. With greater technology and an emphasis on the youth culture, more than ever, teens have greater power to impact society.

So it started with a vision, but the amazing thing is that God went way beyond our vision.

> [20] Now to Him who is able to do immeasurably more than all we ask or imagine, according to His power that is at work within us. (Ephesians 3:20)

On November 14, 2009, we lived this verse of Scripture. God literally connected five times the number of people we were imagining and brought them together to bring Him glory!

Unity Across Denominations

We live in a divided society. Our churches often function in division and separation as well, instead of unity. But this division is not God's will. The body of Christ is supposed to work in unity and power. Let's look at a few Scriptures that teach us about unity.

> [12] Also in Judah the hand of God was on the people to give them unity of mind to carry out what the king and his officials had ordered, following the word of the LORD. (2 Chronicles 30:12)

Psalm 133

A song of ascents. Of David.

[1] How good and pleasant it is
when brothers live together in unity!
[2] It is like precious oil poured on the head,
running down on the beard,
running down on Aaron's beard,
down upon the collar of his robes.
[3] It is as if the dew of Hermon
were falling on Mount Zion.
For there the LORD bestows his blessing,
even life forevermore.

[5]May the God who gives endurance and encouragement give you a spirit of unity among yourselves as you follow Christ Jesus, [6] so that with one heart and mouth you may glorify the God and Father of our Lord Jesus Christ. (Romans 15:5-6)

[11]It was he who gave some to be apostles, some to be prophets, some to be evangelists, and some to be pastors and teachers, [12] to prepare God's people for works of service, so that the body of Christ may be built up [13] until we all reach unity in the faith and in the knowledge of the Son of God and become mature, attaining to the whole measure of the fullness of Christ. (Ephesians 4:11-13)

[14] And over all these virtues put on love, which binds them all together in perfect unity. [15] Let the peace of Christ rule in your hearts, since as members of one body you were called to peace. And be thankful. (Colossians 3:14-15)

From this short list of Scriptures, we can see that unity is something that God expects to see in the body of Christ, and also something that releases power! Christ is the unifying factor that should be the bridge for believers from every nation, tongue, and background.

Unity is what we saw first in New York City and in many cities since. We have seen different churches and teens from all cultures and ethnicities come together, being unified through Jesus Christ. It is amazing how we can talk about people getting along, healing racial tensions, and walking in unity, but it never happens. ***GBIMC*** has proved to be the rallying call that has achieved these goals that often seem unreachable.

Relationships Built

We have seen so many people connect on social and ministry levels. So many leaders and teens live isolated lives when it shouldn't be that way! God created us for relationships and to encourage one another!

[24] And let us consider how we may spur one another on toward love and good deeds. [25] Let us not give up meeting together, as some are in the habit of

doing, but let us encourage one another. (Hebrews 10:24-25a)

In a culture that often isolates or is hostile toward people of committed faith, one of the benefits of ***GBIMC*** is that teens have connected with hundreds of other youth of strong Christian faith. They have met people from their communities from all different cultures, backgrounds, and denominations, promoting diversity. Through this many have been given the opportunity to see and live Christianity in a more powerful way and in community as it should be! The body of Christ is a community of people united by a love for Christ, with people who are just like us and others who are different. This has helped many grow as they have been encouraged by others.

From the Isolated Youth Group to the Body of Christ

Many youth ministries who lacked relationships with other churches have connected in their neighborhoods. This has led to churches and youth ministries supporting each other and working together because of ***GBIMC***.

Too many of our youth ministries have functioned in isolation for too long! Some churches have been so preoccupied with doctrine and ministry style that they have created an atmosphere where teens don't want to be. We totally believe in sound doctrine and in living God's Word, but many church leaders have unnecessarily lived in fear. Our experience has been that it is only the churches that strongly hold to God's Word that are able to work together with other like-minded churches, regardless of minor doctrinal differences or ministry styles.

Many leaders have been paralyzed in the area of partnering with other churches and ministries as they have been afraid of their teens "catching" bad doctrine. Jesus wasn't concerned about catching something; He was too busy spreading something—the Gospel!

Schools Changed

As teens committed to praying in their schools, as a follow-up to the ***GBIMC*** marches, the atmosphere of schools began to change. As teens wore their ***GBIMC*** T-shirts and began to pray in hallways, a sense of godly respect took hold in certain schools. Some schools had many teens praying. One school had one young man kneel in his hallway and pray. It was amazing to see the respect that the entire hallway gave him as he prayed.

Too many people assume that teens don't want or respect God. We have witnessed the opposite of this time after time.

Teens Just Want Something Real!

GBIMC has become an opportunity for real teens to share real faith! When teens begin to pray and speak about the love, power, and purposes of Jesus, other teens listen. When teens are real about their faith, they don't need to be obnoxious or unnecessarily confrontational; they just have to be real and others respond. Many have been encouraged when they find out that so many of their classmates and people in their school also serve Jesus. Can I say, "contagious?"

Taking Action: List some other churches and youth ministries that you can hang out with and do things for Jesus together!

1) ______________________________
2) ______________________________
3) ______________________________

Chapter 9

Aftereffects of GBIMC Prayer Walks

It is hard to really explain how inspired I was on that rainy day. It was the recharge I was personally looking for and it fueled a desire that had been in me long ago. So all I can say is, what's next?

—Rachel-Anne Morales

The aftereffects of the ***God Belongs In My City*** marches have been incredible. Many teens have begun to experience Jesus and life in a greater way. Jesus said:

> I have come that they may have life, and have it to the full. (John 10:10b)

For too many teens who have spent time in church, Jesus' statement has seemed like an empty promise. They haven't experienced that fullness and abundant life that Jesus came to give them. ***GBIMC*** has helped thousands of teens experience the power of prayer and the presence of God in greater ways!

Not Ashamed of the Gospel

One of the greatest aftereffects of the ***God Belongs In My City*** marches has been an increased boldness to share the Gospel. When teens step out to be used by God, He pours His Holy Spirit and power into them! The timid teen now becomes bold for Christ!

> [7]" For God did not give us a spirit of timidity, but a spirit of power, of love and of self-discipline." (2 Timothy 1:7)

I have often said that the more we pour out, the more God pours into us. When teens pray and cry out for their generation, God meets them and gives more of Himself to them.

The Couch, Remote Control, and a Bag of Chips

Unfortunately, for too many teens, all they want out of life is a couch, a TV, and a bowl of snacks! They have prayed and faithfully believed for these and once they have gotten them, either from God or by whining repetitively to their parents, they are satisfied and don't want anything more out of life! I have used this example and often challenged teens to want more than this! If this is all you want from life, it may be all you ever get!

God Answers the Need

When you begin to publicly pray and share Jesus, it creates a demand on your strength, emotions, and spirit. As you pour out to others and the work of God, you will exhaust your limited ability and demonstrate your need for God. When you do this, He shows up!

If you don't pour out spiritually and of yourself, God won't show up in power because there is no need. You already have your big comfy couch, remote control, and bowl of chips. No need for anything else! But at the end of the day, you hear the familiar cry of, "I'm bored," because there is no adventure in sitting around and doing nothing for God! You need to show some passion and get ready for God's passion to work in you and through you! Jesus was bold in His love for you; will you be bold in your love for Him?

Teens Are Bold About Those They Love!

Teens are very passionate and expressive about those they love and care about. Whether it is their friends, boyfriend, girlfriend, or people they don't even know, like singers or movie stars, they passionately defend and promote them! If you are in love with Jesus, you should have this same boldness for Him!

[16] I am not ashamed of the gospel, because it is the power of God for the salvation of everyone who believes: first for the Jew, then for the Gentile. (Romans 1:16)

Larger, More Passionate Youth Ministries

Many youth ministries have grown once their teens have been fired up because of their answered prayers and increased intimacy with Jesus. When teens are fired up about Jesus, it becomes contagious! Many begin to share this passion with both teens that have walked away from the church and new teens who haven't yet heard the Gospel clearly explained.

Changed Atmosphere

Many churches and youth ministries have been impacted in a way that changes the spiritual atmosphere in their churches. As teens have grown in their prayer and worship lives, God's presence has been stronger in many churches and youth group meetings. Real life change takes place and an atmosphere of expectation grows when teens want to bring their friends!

Wearing GBIMC T-shirts in School

About one thousand teens began wearing their ***GBIMC*** T-shirts to school. Some began wearing them every Monday. Others launched the ***"I Am My School"*** prayer movement that encourages teens to take responsibility for their school instead of being disengaged or blaming others for its problems.

Churches and Youth Groups Being Activated

Some churches began to get behind both the ***GBIMC*** and ***"I Am My School"*** movements as they began to adopt schools in their communities to pray for them. On Saturday, students and leaders would go to a school and pray for it. On Sunday, the entire church would pray for the same school. Then on Monday, the teens would wear their ***GBIMC*** T-shirts and pray for their school.

Teachers Getting on Board with GBIMC

While public school teachers can't openly pray and share Christ with students, many Christian teachers pray daily for their students. Many teachers also come out to our ***GBIMC*** prayer walks and encourage the students when they wear their T-shirts. This has also improved the atmosphere of many schools.

The Bible Challenge

One of the greatest affects of the ***GBIMC*** movement is that it encourages many people to do things they would never have done for Christ. Some youth groups have started "The Bible Challenge," where students are challenged to walk around with their Bible in school and on the street. This has caused many to grow in their faith as they read their Bible more and have to answer the questions and challenges of classmates and people on the street.

Taking Action: What are you willing to do differently so that you can live differently?

____

____

____

____

____

____

____

____

____

____

____

____

____

____

Chapter 10

GBIMC—
Spreading to Other Cities

For the past decade, Baltimore has been one of the top five most-violent cities in the United States due to gang violence and drugs. My family, alongside many others in Baltimore, has continually served the community and prayed for change to take place. Within a few years, the homicide rates in Baltimore City have considerably dropped! We don't think this is just a coincidence; we know that God is working in our city. Everyone knows you can never have enough prayer, so when we heard about God Belongs In My City, we really wanted to have one in Baltimore.

Both young and old gathered from all over Baltimore with the same thing in mind: to pray for change. God had made the perfect day for prayer walking. We went from our starting points and began praying for the city. Some of the areas we walked and prayed for were Johns Hopkins and for the policemen that serve in our city. We walked and prayed until we got in front of City Hall, where we formed a circle and prayed for our government. This was really awesome to see! People praying for their city and giving it to God without any interruptions from Satan! Prayer is really important to any city, and in Baltimore, it really seems to be making a difference.

—Josh Stevens, Baltimore

God Belongs In My City wasn't created to go to other cities or to even be an ongoing thing. It was meant to be one day of prayer for one city, but God had other ideas. As news began to spread about the passion of teens to pray for their city, others began to catch the vision. God wants to use teens to change their city. God belongs in every city and He wants to use teens to be His messengers and prayer warriors!

One thing about this youth generation is that you can't force them to do things. If they don't want to do something, they won't! You may be able to get them to do something small, but teens are not going to prepare for weeks, call/text and message friends, and spend a Saturday publicly praying if they haven't caught the vision from God. One of the reasons we wrote this book is so that any teen in any city can pick it up and catch the vision that God has for their city! Any teen, youth pastor, or leader can grab a hold of God's will to change their city and run with it.

Let's Go Viral—In a Good Way!

Just think about this for a second. So many things are being spread virally—both in the natural and spiritual—that are negative. People are spreading sexual diseases, viruses on the Internet, and all other kinds of nonsense. Let's spread something good! You have the ability to spread the Gospel and prayer movements like ***God Belongs In My City*** over the Internet, on smartphones, YouTube, etc., to change the world.

AIDS has become a worldwide disease and has in fact crippled entire countries because of its spread. AIDS is literally spread one person at a time by someone who takes deliberate actions and infects someone else. In the same way, you can deliberately affect one person at a time by purposefully taking action and sharing something with them! You can share the Good News of Jesus deliberately and spread the Gospel one person at a time through your prayers, words, and actions.

In the same way that one person with AIDS who spreads it to another doesn't see how they impact their city and country, what you do has a cumulative effect. There are countries where hundreds of thousands and even millions of children have no parents because they are dead from AIDS. What an amazing thing if the cumulative effects of you and your friends transformed society positively with the message of Christ!

Spread the Cure!

Jesus is the cure! Spiritually, emotionally, intellectually, and physically, He is the cure. In a little over a year, what began as a one-day prayer walk started by four youth leaders from a local church in Brooklyn, ***GBIMC*** has spread around the United States and even to other countries. These include:

New York, NY – November 14, 2009
Baltimore, Maryland – April 10, 2010
Kissimmee, Florida – April 10, 2010
Cleveland, Ohio – May 8, 2010
Orlando, Florida – July 17, 2010
Camden, New Jersey – August 14, 2010
Chicago, Illinois – October 23, 2010
Philadelphia, Pennsylvania – April 2, 2011
New Port Richey, Florida – May 21, 2011
Miami, Florida – June 4, 2011
Hernando County, Florida – June 25, 2011
Ottawa, Canada – July 1, 2011
Puerto Rico – July 16, 2011
Indiana – August 6, 2011
Sayreville, New Jersey – August 13, 2011
Lehigh Valley, Pennsylvania – August 27, 2011
Buffalo, New York – September 2011
Jacksonville, Florida – September 3, 2011
San Antonio, Texas – September 10, 2011
Newark, New Jersey – September 17, 2011
New York City, NY – October 29, 2011
Houston, Texas – November 12, 2011
Dallas, Texas – December 10, 2011
Everywhere else – (Coming soon. Waiting for your response to the call.)

Over twenty thousand T-shirts have been sold all over the United States and several other countries and are being worn by youth and adults declaring that ***God Belongs In My City!*** The ***GBIMC*** prayer movement continues to grow and touch thousands of people on a regular basis.

Social Network Systems Are Neutral

Social network systems are neutral, but people aren't! What you do and say each day makes a difference in our world. When you go on Facebook and text each day, you communicate something. Everything you communicate will either bring people closer to Jesus or push them further away.

> [21]" The tongue has the power of life and death. (Proverbs 18:21a)

Your words have power. Each day, you encourage people to do something. You may influence them to encourage others, or gossip and tear people down. You may encourage them to be bold about their faith, or to sit around and play video games all day. You may encourage them to pursue a relationship with Jesus, or be consumed with their next boyfriend or girlfriend, who will consume them for the next three months, before they move on to the next one!

What you pray (or don't pray) also makes a difference. We've talked a lot about the power of prayer. But understand that if you don't pray, what you don't pray about won't happen! I am convinced that the problems of the world are not just the results of evil people's actions, but mainly the result of the lack of prayers of Christians! Sinners sin; that's what they do. Thieves steal and liars lie. It is only the power of the cross that turns liars and thieves into people who are positive world changers.

Go to God About People Before You Go to People About God!

It is the hearts and minds that need to change before someone's actions and behaviors change. Only God can change the way people think and act. He does this by changing people from the inside out. All of man's best efforts try to change people from the outside in. But over time, unless there is real change on the inside, people go back to the old way they did things, and often bad behaviors and choices get worse.

We often experience the hardness of people's hearts and get frustrated when the reality is, we never prayed for them or asked God to soften and open their hearts. It is God's will that people's hearts and minds are open to Him, so let's pray God's will and then share the message of the cross in a way that they will receive!

Taking Action: Take a prayer walk!

Walk through you town or city and pray for the people, the businesses, the police, the guys hanging out on the corner, and whatever else is on your heart.

Bring a friend or go with your youth group!

Dream! Can you imagine hundreds of youth praying for your city? What does it look like?

Chapter 11

Pray in Your School; Pray for Your School!

But I'm only fifteen; what can I do? OK—enough already with the nonsense about being too young, too this, or too that. You are filled with the Spirit of God and can do all things through Christ who strengthens you! That is your reality; you can either accept it or reject it! You can either walk in it or sit on your couch and play Xbox until your brain freezes up!

God Belongs In My City T-Shirts—Every Monday in School

Our teens began to wear their ***GBIMC*** T-shirts every Monday and prayed that God would begin to change their classmates, teachers, coaches, and administrators! They made a bold statement and God honored it!

Give God Something to Bless!

God is looking for people to strengthen and to bless!

> [9] For the eyes of the LORD range throughout the earth to strengthen those whose hearts are fully committed to him. (2 Chronicles 16:9a)

It amazes me how God wants to strengthen us. The Lord is in heaven, and His eyes are gazing across our country and throughout our cities, searching for someone to strengthen. When He strengthens us, we can do all things! (Philippians 4:13) You just have to commit your heart totally to Him!

Teens Love Giving Their Hearts Away!

In your schools each day, around town and at the mall, millions of teens are spending their time and energy trying to give their hearts away to somebody, and for some, to anybody! God has wired us to give our hearts away, first to Him and then to others. The reality is that we give away some of our heart to all that we are close and committed to. This includes parents, friends, and for some, the "almighty" boyfriend or girlfriend. Of course I'm joking about the "almighty" boyfriend or girlfriend, but that's how many teens treat their temporary romantic journey/tragedy.

God Wants All of You!

It amazes me to see how many people completely give their hearts away to a person but hold back from God. I once watched a young man slam his girlfriend into a locker, at which time I began to show my displeasure (I began to calmly explain to him what a complete low-life loser he was). In the middle of it, she got in my face for disrespecting him! This beautiful and intelligent young girl had fully given her heart away to a low-life, going nowhere, idiot. Yes, I (Jack) said it, and yes, I mean it. Pray for me too, if needed! At the same time, so many people hold back their heart from God. I have seen many other young women and young men give their hearts to Jesus and be magnificently changed and grow over time.

Will You Stand Up for Jesus?

This young lady was willing to stand up for an abusive boyfriend who was just using her on the way to his next victim, and she boldly stood up to me when I was trying to help her because she cared more about him than herself! Will you have the same or greater boldness to stand up for Jesus? If this young lady can be that bold for that guy, can you be bold for the One who created you and the One who died for you?

Enough with the "I Go to Church" Nonsense

Too many teens go to church to please and keep their parents off their backs, but are not really doing what Jesus commands them to do. Let's be real; too many people that go to church are pathetically weak in the things of God. Hey, while we are being real, there are many adults who are like this. In fact, they've probably been like that since they were teens! Too many people who go to church and consider themselves Christians are the type of people that give the atheists intellectual ammunition to back up their view that God is either powerless or doesn't exist!

God has called you to be salt and light and a world changer! Don't you want to live an amazing life and do amazing things for Jesus? Don't you want to see Jesus miraculously change your friend's life? It's up to you. If you have truly committed to following Jesus and are born again, the same Holy Spirit that raised Jesus Christ from the dead lives inside of you! It's now up to you to walk in that resurrection power in your life and to share it with others.

We challenge you to pray each day for your city, and if God is leading you to start to put together a group of teens to pray for your school and city, then go for it! If you really want to make it happen, you can start to gather teens, youth ministries, and leaders together where you live. How do I do that? I thought you'd never ask—lol! Just keep reading....

Taking Action: Make a prayer list for your school. What do you want to see God change?

People: ______________________________

____

Things: ______________________________

____

Chapter 12

GBIMC—
Adaptable to Any City—
Adaptable to YOUR City!

Jesus Had Twelve to Walk the Cities

Jesus had twelve main disciples, and He walked with them through the city streets and they changed the world! You can walk the streets and pray by yourself each and every day! You can also join with others for additional and different types of prayers, each bringing change to different concerns in your city.

Key Steps to Holding a GBIMC Prayer Walk

1) **A leader with vision:** God is always looking to partner with people to work in them and through them.

This always begins with someone who sees what God wants to do and begins to connect with and lead other people. Whether you are the main leader, an assistant, or someone who serves or participates doesn't matter as much as just doing your part. But somewhere on the team, there must be someone who is the point person.

2) **Casting the vision:** A clear vision of the event and goals must be shared so that people understand what they are being asked to be a part of so they can fully commit. It must be grassroots in its organization and how things happen. ***GBIMC*** doesn't exist to oversee and hold prayer walks, but to share the vision and give the tools to empower local groups of leaders to lead and hold prayer walks for "their" city!

3) **Organizer/Administrator:** This person's role is to help administer various aspects such as planning meetings, setting dates, and collect and manage T-shirt money. They make things happen on an ongoing basis. This may be the visionary leader, but it helps to have different people with special gifts serving on the team.

4) **Connect and meet with others:** Most teams usually meet three to four times to prepare for a ***GBIMC*** walk. Purposely reach out to diverse church groups, backgrounds, denominations, and neighborhoods in your city. The goal is not to agree on every doctrinal issue or style of ministry, but to connect with people who truly

love and serve Jesus Christ and are committed to living out the Bible and mandates of Jesus. As long as we agree on the major issues, we cannot get overly concerned about the details that unnecessarily divide us at times.

5) **List specific needs of your city:** These needs can be circulated and prayed about before, during, and after the ***GBIMC*** prayer walk.

6) **Focus on the needs of youth instead of church politics, etc.:** Keep it about Jesus—not about drama!

7) **Purposely engage and include youth:** To truly succeed in the ***GBIMC*** prayer walk, it must be embraced and driven by the youth. Too many youth activities are adult-driven and we just invite the kids to come along! This is not what we are after. We want teens who embrace the responsibility to pray for their generation!

8) **Use Technology and Network**
   a. Create e-mail distribution lists for quick communication
   b. Create a Facebook group for your city and assign one or more administrators
   c. Create YouTube clips
   d. Make personal phone calls to key leaders and churches

9) **Invite adults to take part:** While the goal is to be youth-driven, you will need adult buy-in and support from youth leaders, senior pastors, and community members for maximum impact.

10) **Schedule a day—usually one to three months out from initial meeting**

11) **Follow up**
    a. Celebrate accomplishments—YouTube clips, etc.
    b. Continue relationships to support each other and events
    c. Continue wearing T-shirts to school and in neighborhoods

Keys to Getting Teens to Buy In

1) Show ***GBIMC*** video to grab the attention and get teens interested.
2) Teach on prayer—its importance and how to do it in real life.
3) Have teens lead prayer in your youth services and events.
4) Give teens a prayer focus to pray about throughout the week and to help establish a lifestyle of prayer.
5) Teach teens to look at society—in daily life, on the Internet, news, etc., to look for issues to pray about.

6) Help teens build strong relationships with each other and adults, to stay connected to youth ministry, church, and the body of Christ.
7) Constantly remind teens that their prayers are powerful and effective and change lives!

Praying for Our Cities!

When we pray, lives and cities can be changed. Remember the directions God gave to His people when they were exiled in Babylon:

> Also, seek the peace and prosperity of the city to which I have carried you into exile. Pray to the LORD for it, because if it prospers, you too will prosper. (Jeremiah 29:7)

Remember that God never changes! He wanted His people to pray for the city they lived in then, and He wants His people to pray for the city they live in now. As God's people pray, He moves on their behalf and lives and cities are changed. God belongs in your city. He inhabits the praises of His people and He gets involved in our situations and cities if we invite Him in through prayer!

God wants to do more in our personal lives and in our cities than we can think or even imagine! Let's begin to pray for our cities in greater ways and expect God to transform them. ***God Belongs In My City*** and in yours! Let's join together and pray and see God not only change our cities, but also change our nation and our world!

Won't you join us and pray? Won't you pray? Won't you help us change our nation?

Taking Action: Start writing down the people and things you need to do to have a ***GBIMC*** **Prayer Walk**. Look at it as a working list that is changeable as different people get involved. Just start the process and see what God will do!

1) **A leader with vision:** ______________________
2) **Casting the vision:** ______________________
3) **Organizer/Administrator:**______________________
4) **Connect and meet with others:**
    a. Who ______________________
    b. Where/When ______________________

5) **List specific needs of your city:**
    a. ______________________
    b. ______________________
    c. ______________________

6) **Key Youth:**
    a. ______________________
    b. ______________________

7) **Use Technology and Network—who will take care of these?**
    a. E-mail list ______________________
    b. Facebook group ___________________
    c. YouTube clips ____________________
    d. Phone calls ______________________

8) **Key Leaders and Support People:**
    a. ______________________________
    b. ______________________________

9) **Date of GBIMC Prayer Walk:** ______________

10) **Follow up**
    a. Celebrate accomplishments—YouTube clips, etc.
    b. Continue relationships to support each other and events
    c. Continue wearing T-shirts to school and in neighborhoods

God wants to change your city! He is looking for a few faithful who can lead a multitude! You may be a leader or one of the multitude. Either way, it doesn't matter as long as you are part of the team! Team Jesus taking over your city!

To become the movement, contact us directly at 347-760-3008 and we will help you declare that ***"God Belongs In My City!"***

God Belongs In My City—
Let's pray for our cities and change our nation!

Author Contact Information

Jack Redmond
Founder and President of Fourth Generation Ministries
P.O. Box 376
Rockaway, NJ 07866
973-954-4227
www.4thgen.org

Daniel Sanabria
www.Godbelongsinmycity.com
347-760-3008
www.urbankingdomym.com